CONTENTS:
- **Translator's note**
  - **Armand Cherpillod**
  - **Wrestling**

Translator's Note:

It has been my impression that standup wrestling is given short shrift in the martial arts world. Outside of the realm of Judo - standup grappling in a gi - we tend to see the grappling arts as emphasizing the ground game with the occasional insertion of some standup during which the entire dojo must move aside while two players work to take one another down - and therein, perhaps, lies the rub. A lot of gyms offer limited space, their various vertical surfaces are not entirely or adequately padded, and there are a number of people working at various aspects of their own game who will not appreciate having a third party suddenly thrown on top of them. This brings us to the subject of injury, which is certainly more likely to occur with throws, trips, and tumbles. Even with plenty of goodwill, waivers, and legal boilerplate, the owner of a martial arts establishment will always have to fear the possibility of someone being wheeled out in a cervical collar - "so today, folks, let's start from the closed guard…"

But seriously - standing grappling is a really nuanced game, and is fascinating to watch, as we can see from its ongoing appeal, albeit in a theatrical form.

Armand Cherpillod was the real deal, rare sportsman who, having cut his teeth in the tough arena of Swiss folk wrestling, went on to beat catch wrestlers twice his size - even a guy called the "Beef Mountain"! He did this through pure knowhow, and indeed, the man was a wrestling encyclopedia. While the fully free grappling style went into decline and the well-bounded worlds of Greco-Roman and freestyle have been relegated to amateur and collegiate pursuits, a portion of Cherpillod's wisdom lives on within the pages of this manual. It is amazing the amount of knowledge that is lost or discarded for one reason or another, only to be dusted off by another generation, who find in it something which seems utterly new.

Armand Cherpillod

These are the measurements of a normal male, and so he seems to be with his easy gait, even temper, and good nature devoid of pretense. There is nothing in these numbers to hint at his particular gifts, and no one would, at first glance, suppose that Armand Cherpillod was a champion wrestler.

On the 23rd of September, 1901, London's **Bartitsu Club**, in seeking out combat sports champions from around the world, contacted Cherpillod. He had been recommended to them not as the strongest, but as the most skilled of Swiss wrestlers, and as such he was made that society's professor of fitness and grappling.

England, the center of the world for all of those deemed worthy of celebrity status, became the stage for the greatest exploits of our valorous countryman. From wrestling championships organized in 1901 and 1902 in Oxford, Cambridge, Glasgow, Liverpool, Newcastle, Dublin, Nottingham, Manchester, Sandgate, Birmingham and London, Cherpillod emerged undefeated.

Named the British champion on 11 December 1901, Armand capped it all in being proclaimed the World Champion by the *National Sporting Club* following matches organized in June of 1902. That same organization made him an honorary member at an event held in the Convent Gardens for the crowning of his majesty Edward VII. In just two days he defeated 18 wrestlers from around the world, the lightest of which weighed no less than 192 lbs. The spectators, mainly the nobility of England and Europe, crowded his award ceremony and offered enthusiastic applause.

Amid all of these honors he never forgot his beloved Swiss homeland,   and before long his *Heimweh* or homesickness brought him back. There he took up residence in Sainte-Croix. Far from resting on his laurels, he went on to win the canton-wide festival at Vaudoise à l'Aigle (1902) and the International Contest at Besançon (1902), before being named "Champion of France" at the Olympic games.

He returned to England in 1904 and took part in 3 championships from which he emerged the victor: The lightweight category which contained 72 wrestlers, the heavyweight category with 116, and the Royal Club grouping with its 45 wrestlers.

Returning home he only took part in various local festivals and served on some juries, but even then we were able to marvel at his knowledge.

In 1905 he defeated the Danish lightweight Lauritz Nielsen in 2 rounds, the first lasting 17 minutes and the next only 33 seconds.

Recently he was called upon to give wrestling instruction to the Royal Marines in Portsmouth, where the naval command bestowed high praise and honors upon him.

He again earned the title of World Champion (heavyweight) of the City of London.

But the most epic battle Cherpillod ever faced was in 1905 when he took on the giant Grumley. Nicknamed "The Beef Mountain" by the English, this gigantic grappler stands 1m 97 tall and weighs 120 kilos. He was named World Champion at Edinburgh and then in India some months before, but he struggled against Cherpillod in vain. In two consecutive matches, one being 30 minutes long and the other 15, the Swiss master used his skill to gain a brilliant victory over his terrible adversary.

And yet all the world would repeat the refrain: "He just doesn't have that look about him!" All of the tough guys who were bigger, meaner, stronger and heavier than him would make the same error, but for them the mistake was consequential, in that it would end with them being slammed to their backs in disbelief. As for Armand, he was always the same guy despite his success: Humble and modest, an utter stranger to bravado.

Indeed, Cherpillod is the very embodiment of the Swiss character, combining immovable calm, incomparable tenacity, and the greatest power within the least space: A human battery, full of energy.

His finely proportioned body leaves him with the greatest possible scope for movement. His neck is not too short nor is his head buried among big shoulders as is the case with so many athletes. His well maintained torso is not over-developed and his lungs seem to be able to provide infinite oxygen. The proof of this can be found in one 2 minute, 6 second match against a powerful opponent: Joe Carrol, a well known grappler who had held the title of "Champion of England" for 8 years - and had been undefeated until his meeting with Cherpillod.

Each of us knows that some solid qualities must come together in order for a man to surpass all competitors in any given domain. With this in mind the life of Cherpillod merits some study, both in terms of biographical interest and in terms of the use we might derive from the information.

First let it be said that Armand attributes his robustness to the air and the water of Sainte-Croix. The development of his lungs is doubtless the result of having to trek to school in all kinds of weather, and then when he was 19 he would make a daily trip to the factory at which he worked: This was a 15 minute hike *with a 200 meter vertical rise*. As he walked, be it uphill or down, Armand had the habit of singing in a full throated manner.

For those who consider muscular strength to be purely the product of nutrition, here are some guidelines: Cherpillod was raised on mother's milk until the age of 2, and then for many years he took cafe au lait and black bread morning and evening, with a lunch of soup and vegetables supplemented with a bit of lard or some other meat product. Throw in some additional milk and fruit, and you have the entire diet of his youth.

He went about climbing the ranks, slowly and without shocks, until at last he earned the coveted and hotly disputed title of World Champion.

Most people who attend a wrestling match believe that victory will go to the strongest: This is a basic error. Cherpillod has proven this abundantly, and he will tell you the story of the oaktree and the reed, then speak in detail about the astonishing power of Japanese wrestling which relies entirely upon flexibility and agility. In the field of wrestling as in all others it is these two qualities, combined with cunning, which can vanquish brute power. Bend, withdraw, cede some territory, harass your enemy with disconcerting inertia - but keep a level head, an open mind, a clear eye, an exact notion of space and time. Even if you're upside down, know how to profit from the smallest errors your opponent will surely make. All of this taken together constitutes a force which is more formidable than brute strength: **Art.** Cherpillod is the representative of the **Art** of wrestling above all else.

-Oscar Campiche, 1905.

Wrestling

Wrestling dates back to the most ancient times, and is likely the most primitive exercise among all peoples, with only specific rules and customs differing from one land to the next. It has the advantage of developing the body in a normal and balanced manner since it brings into play all of the muscles of the human mechanism, and it is also a marvelous means of self defense which is not to be disdained. Wrestling is the most complete sport, since it demands considerable physical effort, strength of will, and above all agility. It also calls for a level head, and through this it can place the spirit in harmony with bodily strength, stamina, and the intellect.

Grappling does not have to be a brutal and dangerous game. It has nothing in common with street self-defense systems, rather it is a pure sport that is elegant and courteous. Among friends a session must remain civil, and when we bring an opponent to the ground we go along with him in order to avoid injuries. If in the pages of this manual we have described a large number of techniques which bring us down to the mat, it is only with the intention of pursuing victory from there while avoiding injury. Once a wrestler has made several attempts to submit his opponent, we urge students not to remain on the ground contesting the matter but to rise up and resume standing grappling, as this is always the most favorable use of time.

In free wrestling, which is the subject we are here addressing, takedowns, trips, and sweeps are allowed. This is the kind of grappling we tend to favor, and it is the most natural sort of competition since it keeps every muscle group engaged and allows for the entire body to become more fully trained. We make use of all of the natural weapons which are not allowed in Greco-Roman wrestling, where you are prohibited from attacking the legs or grabbing the opponent below the belt. Free wrestling therefore makes use of upper body holds, lower body holds, and mixed holds (with one hand or arm above the belt and one below). If a competitor makes use of a mixed hold or a lower body hold he is looking to lift his opponent in order to then bring him down.

In some systems victory is determined by one competitor keeping the other man's shoulder blades flat on the mat for a determined time. In Switzerland the measure of success is to bring some portion of the opponent's upper body to the ground, be it his back, neck, shoulders, or buttocks.

Before an audience wrestlers ought to appear in proper garb, including wrestling slippers, socks, long pants, a shirtsleeves, or such costumes as are worn in gymnastic exercises.

It is essential for players to take a 2 or 3 hour rest after meals and before taking part in grappling. It is true that at exhibitions time can be quite limited, and for this reason rest periods are often difficult to insert. In any event we recommend that wrestlers do not eat much before giving themselves over to training.

The duration of a match should not exceed 10 minutes which is enough time to appreciate what two competitors are capable of doing.

Once a match is done a wrestler should neither sit down nor lay down, but to the contrary, it is better to spend some time walking around slowly in order to allow the muscles to wind down by degrees. Through this measure we are also looking to avoid any circulatory disturbances. After training it is also best to give the most hard-working muscle groups a rubdown, and when a shower is available one should never pass up the opportunity.

When wrestling you should avoid leaving the mouth open as this can lead to hyperventilation: Breath in slowly through the nose and exhale freely through the mouth. Only regular training (1 or 2 lessons per week) will impart the ability to remain calm during combat while conserving presence of mind. Never get worked up, but to the contrary, keep a level head and only go on the offensive when the time is ripe.

Sobriety is the rule and alcohol must be set aside - smoking as well. At competitions over the past few years we have seen that the choice to replace wine with some hot tea has been well received by professional athletes.

We don't want to be repetitive - our techniques can be used to the left or to the right, as we are sure our readers will easily understand.

As you will see from the images, **A** is usually the attacker and **B** is the one receiving the technique.

Without extensive explanation the reader will comprehend how one will be able to employ a technique against a larger or smaller opponent with success.

When attacked one must rotate swiftly and seek to face the opponent. Such turns are very useful in order to insure that you will land on your back when taken down, as opposed to landing in a prone position.

We have put aside - we do not recommend - the head throw as a counter to a rear belt, and the same goes for the reverse belt, as both of these techniques are prone to producing injury.

In a wrestling class, if the participants are numerous it is best to place them in two groups. Instructors should break a technique down into component steps with care, with one group applying the technique while the other receives it, and then switch.

At seminars we have seen groups who undertake wrestling exercises in a choreographed sequence and this produces excellent results.

-E. Richème & G. Desauges

One.
Handshake:

The opponents shake hands before and after each engagement in order to call to mind that there is an underlying courtesy which reigns between competitors in wrestling, whatever the end result might be.

Two.

Guard:

    After the handshake the opponents withdraw by a few paces and assume the guard. The torso leans forward ever so slightly while the arms are bent and the elbows are held not too far from the body. The hands are open and the eyes take in the whole of the opponent's form.

Three.
Takedown:

    A feigns a high-line attack before lowering his stance quickly in order to seize the opponent by the backs of his knees. He pulls **B** towards him while pushing with his left shoulder in order to topple player **B** directly backwards. **A**'s head can also be to the left.

    To counter this motion, **B** wraps **A** up in both arms (i.e. belting him) from the rear and leans back.

Four.

Leg Grab:

    A feigns a high line attack and lowers his stance quickly in order to snatch **B**'s left leg from the outside at the level of the ankle. **A** stands up bringing the leg with him, placing his left hand or forearm on the opponent's chest to push him back. Player **B** is toppled backward. To counter this motion **B** should turn quickly and seize either the arm or the head of the attacker.

Five.

Front belt & inside hook:

A wraps player **B** up in a belt around his lower back, then brings his right leg between those of **B** and hooks the left leg. **A** rotates to the left and topples **B** over, though **B** can also be sent straight back.

Six.

Immediate counter to the front belt with an inside hook:

Belt the opponent from the front and hook his leg as with the prior technique. Here, player **B** will raise his left leg in order to trap player **A**'s hooking leg. **B** now places his right hand on the left arm of **A** at the tricep, pulling him in while spinning hard to the right.

Seven.
Counter the front belt with an inside hook:
(A mixed hold with the left arm high and the right arm low)

    A belts **B** with his left arm high and his right arm low, then hooks his leg as is indicated in technique 5. **B** now belts **A** with his right arm while with his left hand he seizes **A**'s right leg at the instep. **B** now blocks **A**'s left heel with his left foot and spins to the left (release the foot upon his fall).

Eight.

Inside hook with a belt counter:

See the first and second steps of the prior technique. Now **B** should counter by passing his right leg between those of the opponent, placing his foot behind **A**'s left leg while pushing with the right shoulder.

Nine.

Inside hook with forearm pressure:

A uses his right leg to hook **B**'s left leg from the inside, placing his right forearm beneath the opponent's chin with his right hand going to **B**'s right shoulder. **A** grabs the right arm with his left hand, then pulls the left leg of **B** towards him while exerting pressure with his forearm. From the position indicated above, player **A** can move on to arm throws (see 18 & 19).

Ten.

Leg grab with inside hook:

    A seizes the right leg of **B** with his left arm on the outside and his right arm on the inside. **A** then hooks the left leg of **B** with his right leg. **A** lifts the right leg of **B** and pushes with his left shoulder.

Player **A** grabs the right thigh of **B** with his right arm on the outside and his left arm on the inside. He then takes his right leg which is slightly bent to the outside of the left leg of player **B**, raising **B**'s right leg while allowing himself to spin to the right.

Instead of seizing the thigh with both arms, player **A** can belt player **B** with his right arm while passing it under the left arm of **B**.

Instead of belting with his right arm, player **A** can opt for a hold above the shoulder or even a rear head hook (see 62).

This move can also be applied after an arm drag as is indicated in the counter in 65.

Twelve.

Belt and an outside cross hook:

    Player **A** belts **B** with his right arm and takes control of **B**'s right arm with his own left arm. He passes his right leg outside of **B**'s right leg such that **B** is toppled directly backwards or taken down by a rotation to the left.

With his right arm **A** seizes the head of **B**, and with his left hand he grabs B's right arm. **A** turns his back to **B**, passes his right leg to the outside of the right leg of **B,** and continues by leaning forward with a leftward rotation.

Fourteen.
Head and arm throw:

The same mechanics of the prior technique, but here **B** is simply loaded onto the hip (without the use of the trip) and taken over the top.

As with the prior technique, but instead of seizing the head with the right arm, **A** belts the opponent's hips.

Sixteen.
Hip & arm throw, underhooked:

Just as with the preceding technique but instead of belting the opponent with his right arm player **A** sends his right arm under **B**'s armpit and takes control of his right arm.

It is best if **A** captures the right arm of **B** and maintains his upper arm in the armpit rather than the shoulder proper. In order to ease his opponent's fall **A** would do well to drop to his right knee so as to go to the mat with **B**.

If A fails to load **B** up properly, he can overhook **B**'s right thigh or shove it with his right hand as shown in figures 46 & 47.

Seventeen.

Hip throw using an overhooked arm:

Just as in the previous technique, but instead of passing his right arm under **B**'s arm, **A** over-hooks the right arm of **B**.

Eighteen.

Overhook arm drag and leg sweep:

Just as with the prior technique, but instead of loading the opponent onto his hip, **A** passes his leg to the outside in order to sweep **B**'s right leg, detaching it from the floor. **A** sends **B** to his back with a strong rotation to his left.

Nineteen.

Overhook arm drag with a trip:

Same as the prior technique, save that instead of sweeping his leg outward **A** merely passes it to the right and brings some of the opponent's weight onto his hip, pulling **B** to him while executing a strong rotation to the left.

Twenty.
Underhook arm drag & trip:

Same as the prior technique, except that here the arm of player **B** is trapped from beneath by player **A**.

If **B** offers too much resistance such that his balance cannot be broken, **A** drops to his right knee while sliding his right hand to control **B**'s forearm and to gain a greater degree of rotation. In falling to his knee, **A** can also conserve his hold on the opponent's upper arm.

Twenty Two.

Trip with a reverse head hold:

Just as in 18, 19, and 20, but instead of over-hooking or under-hooking **B**'s right arm, **A** passes his arm around the back of **B**'s head.

Twenty Three.

Arm drag with outside hook & upper body pressure:

Just as in 18 and 19, but instead of relying upon a rotation, player **A** will hook **B**'s leg from the outside and exert pressure with his upper body in order to force **B** over. This technique is applied while throwing oneself upon the opponent.

Just as in the prior technique, but instead of overhooking the right arm - especially if **B** has his right hand on **A**'s shoulder and plans to encircle the neck - **A** applies pressure to the right arm of **B** and forces him to bend. At this point the arm is trapped, and **B** is taken down either directly backward or through a leftward rotation.

Twenty Five.

Countering the head-and-hip throw with or without a trip:

As soon as **A** takes hold of **B**'s head, the latter belts him and applies his left knee to the back of **A**'s left knee in order to halt his movement. **B** then lifts **A**, toppling him to the left as is indicated in figure 31. Instead of belting the opponent, **B** could place his left hand against the left shoulder blade of **A** (see 27) or even place both hands on **A**'s lower back, applying pressure. Further, **B** could opt to place his left hand on the nape of the opponent's neck and pass in front of him in order to apply a hip throw.

Twenty Six.

Countering the head-and-hip with a trip:

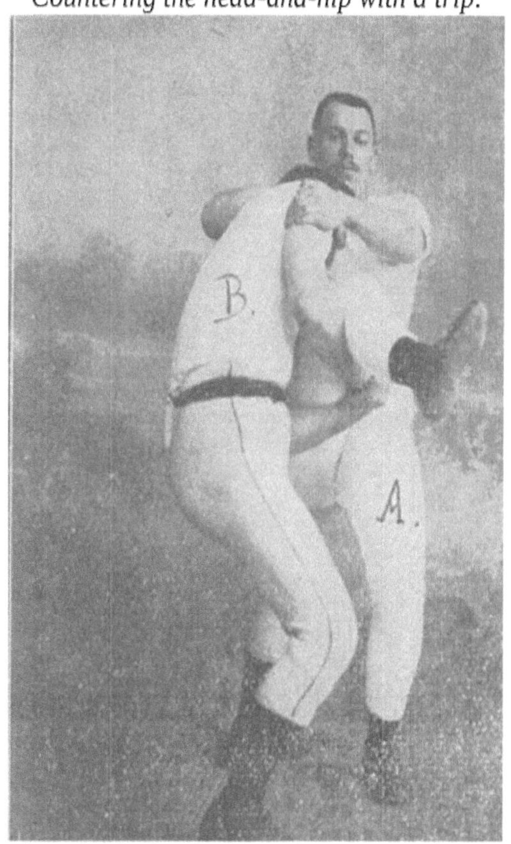

So soon as **A** grabs the head of **B** and tries to apply a trip, **B** underhooks the tripping leg with both hands and lifts it. When this is done with speed, **A** will be sent directly to his back.

Twenty Seven.

Countering an arm throw with or without a trip:

    A attempts to take **B** down as indicated in figures 18 and 19. **B** places his left hand in the middle of the attacker's back, belts him with his right arm and squeezes him against his body. With his left foot he sweeps the left leg of **A** at as low a point as possible while rotating to the left in order to take him down.

Twenty Eight.
Countering an arm throw with a leg hook:

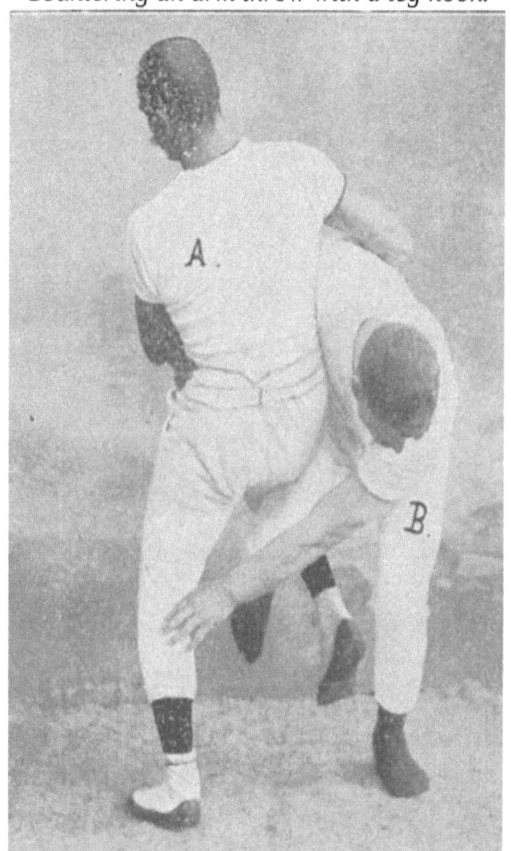

A seeks to topple **B** in the manner shown in 18 and 19. **B** leans down to shove the back of **A**'s knee at the same time, then raises his hooked right leg to force **A**'s own right leg off of the floor, unbalancing him. If **B** falls to his left knee he will have the greatest chance at success.

Twenty Nine.

Countering an arm throw using an outside trip:

   A wants to take **B** down as in 18 and 19. At that moment, **B** spins to the left and places his right leg outside of the left leg of **A** while putting his left hand to **A**'s left shoulder. **B** belts the attacker with his right arm and continues his rotation, briskly toppling **A** over his extended leg.

Direct counter to the arm throw with a hook:

    A seeks to put **B** on his back in the manner shown in 18 and 19. At that moment **B** belts **A** with his right arm, lifts him with the aid of his right shoulder, and raises his bent right leg so as to trap **A**'s hooking leg. He then rotates to the left.

Thirty One.

Counter the arm throw with a hook:

B seeks to topple **A** to his back using an arm throw with a trip. **A** belts him and lifts, so **B** turns his back to the opponent and inserts an outside hook with his left leg to the left leg of his opponent. **A** moves his right arm and places it on the nape of **B**'s neck, then spins to the left and falls to his left side in order to bring his opponent down on his shoulders. One often sees this technique used when **A** attacks with a rear belt, at which point one should proceed in the manner stated above.

Thirty Two.
Countering double outside leg hooks:

Here we have the position described in the previous technique, but **A** and **B** have switched places. With his left hand **B** grabs **A**'s left instep while bending his legs. **A** falls down prone to the mat. Thus freed, **B** turns to the ground fighting techniques found in 87 and beyond.

A seeks to take **B** down in the manner described in 18 and 19. **B** belts **A** and lifts him, squeezing him in hard and delivering a right heel strike to the right foot of **A** in order to detach the hook.

Before removing the right leg of **A**, **B** can wrap the opponent's right thigh with his left arm (inside hook) while his right arm maintains the belt. Further, the right thigh can be grabbed with both arms as in figure 66. After removing **A**'s hook, player **B**, taking care to use the inside hold recommended above, pulls on the hooking leg with his left arm and rotates to the right in order to bring **A** down through a left hip throw by seizing his opponent's left arm with his right hand.

Continuing from the prior technique:

Now that the hook has been detached, **B** lifts **A** in front of him to a horizontal position. **B** grabs **A**'s left hand, arm, or shoulder with his right hand and sends the opponent to his back in front of him. See 69 and 70 as well.

First **A** grabs the wrists of **B**, left hand to left wrist. **B**'s palms face the floor and his left arm crosses over **A**'s right arm, while **A**'s right hand holds **B**'s right wrist in a low position.

Thirty Six.
Continuation of 35.

    Now **A** spins to the left such that **B**'s left arm passes over his head. **A** loads **B** onto his back, dropping to the right as he continues his leftward rotation while sweeping his right leg upward and holding his foot up such that the opponent's leg is trapped.

    Instead of a spin with a kick or sweep, **A** can bring **B** over his head, but this is a dangerous throw which can cause injury.

Thirty Seven.
Reverse headlock with inside corkscrew hook:

    A wraps the head of **B** from above and behind, passing his right leg between those of the opponent. He wraps **B**'s left leg up in a corkscrew manner with his toes coming to **B**'s instep. **A** carefully traps the right arm of **B** with his left hand and spins to the right, leaning back while tensioning his corkscrew hook.

Thirty Eight.
Countering the prior technique:

   A seeks to take **B** down as in 38. **B** immediately belts **A**, passes his own right leg between those of the opponent and delivers a calf sweep to **A**'s right leg. See 8 as well.

A grabs the right arm of **B** as shown in 17, 18 and 19. He passes his bent right leg between those of the opponent and leans well forward while lifting his right leg such that **B** is unbalanced and falls.

This move can be performed with an outside cross sweep or a hook as seen in 18, 19, and 20.

Leg trap with an inside hook:

From the position indicated in the prior technique, **A** releases his arm hold to seize the opponent's right leg as low as possible, lifting it up. The following technique is a counter to this.

Forty One.

Countering the inside leg hook with a crotch lift:

With his right leg **A** applies an inside hook to the left leg of **B** while at the same time seizing his opponent's right leg with his right arm. **B** feels the threat and gets a hold between **A**'s legs, his right arm to the outside. He falls to his right knee while rotating to the right. Before allowing **B** to complete this hold between the legs, **A** can counter **B** in the manner shown in figure 40.

A seeks to implement the crotch lift so **B** passes his right leg between the legs of **A**, hooking the left leg. At the moment when **A** lifts **B**, the latter uses his left hand to grab the ankle of the right foot from the outside in order to detach that foot from the ground.

A applies the crotch lift to **B** as shown in 42. **B** grabs his right leg in order to prevent **A**'s spin to the right which would bring him down. **A** releases his right hand in order to grab the left wrist of **B**. He pulls hard and overturns **B** in front of him. Instead of grabbing the wrist **A** can throw his right leg forward and under the body of **B** while spinning to his right, drawing **B** towards him. This last method of throwing the leg out is recommended above all when the opponent places his hand low at the ankle.

From the position shown in 39, but reversed. **B** sets his left hand on the nape of **A**'s neck while raising his bent right leg in order to trap the hooking leg of **A**. **B** exerts pressure on the head of **A**, raises his right leg as high as possible, and turns to the left.

Defend the arm throw with an inside hook:

From the position shown in 39: **B** feels his left leg getting hooked and stretches his trapped leg out behind him. He uses his right hand to grab **A**'s left arm, and at the same time he grabs the opponent's right leg with his left hand. By pushing forward he forces **A** to withdraw the leg.

For further developments along this line, see 34 and 80 (**B**), 69, 70 and 79 (**A**).

Forty Six.
Arm drag with knee block:

A turns to the right and seeks to make **B** raise his rear foot, his body weight thus coming to his right leg. With his right hand **A** applies an outside block to the right knee of **B**, and with the left hand he grabs the upper right arm. **A** rotates to the left and pushes hard with his right shoulder.

The opponents each have a knee on the mat, and from here **A** works to execute the maneuver indicated in the prior technique.

Forty Eight.
An outside trip with arm hold:

    A passes his right arm under the left arm of **B** while grabbing **B**'s upper right arm with his left hand. **A** blocks out **B**'s right foot with his own right foot from the outside. With his tripping leg firm, **A** rotates to the left while taking a lunging step with his left leg, pulling the opponent hard. This technique requires some muscular exertion.

A rushes B and encircles his lower back while applying his chin to the opponent's chest, forcing him straight back. To counter this front belt you can place either a forearm or hand under the attacker's chin and push. See 65.

Fifty.

Front belt with outside hook:

    A wraps **B** up around the lower back. He then uses his right leg to insert an outside hook to **B**'s left leg. By exerting pressure with his upper body and drawing the hooked leg back, **A** can send **B** to the mat.

A belts B in the manner described above and lifts him in order to load him onto his right hip, then rotates to the left for the takedown.

Just as in the prior technique, save that **A** will put his right thigh between the thighs of **B**, raising his bent leg in order to load the opponent onto his hip more easily.

A belts **B** as indicated in techniques 49, 51, and 52. **B** underhooks the arms of **A** with his forearms in front of his chest, then rotates to the left while applying an outside sweep with his left leg to **A**'s right leg.

Instead of sweeping, a strong and agile wrestler can, once he has encircled the arms of the attacker, give a twist in order to get the opponent off of his feet. From here the attacker may fall or at least end up stumbling to the mat in some way.

Fifty Four.
Body hold with a knee bump:

A grabs **B** around the body, his right arm under the opponent's left and his left arm over it. He places his bent left leg to the outside of **B**'s right leg and applies a knee to it while spinning left to take the opponent backward over his leg. The knee bump described here can also be used with the front belt (see 49).

Fifty Five.
Body hold with a trip (cross outside hook):

As in the prior technique, but here we replace the knee bump with a right leg trip.

Fifty Six.
Body hold plus a thigh to hip throw:

A passes his right arm under the left arm of **B**. With his left hand he grabs the opponent's right thigh, lifts it, loads **B** onto his hip using the gap created between the opponent's thighs, and spins to the right.

This motion can also be employed with the front belt (see 49).

Fifty Seven.
Counter the rear belt:

A takes the back of **B** and belts him. **B** bends down before being lifted
and grabs **A**'s ankle, lifting it high as he returns to a stand, sending **A** to his
back. This must be done before **A** begins his lift, passing his right arm as is
shown in 31.

Fifty Eight.

Counter the reverse belt:

A applies a reverse belt to **B** and the latter grabs both of his wrists, holding them tight to him. **B** then passes his head to the left side of the opponent's torso and overturns him by turning and shoving to the right.

In order to ensure success **B** can drop to his left knee, and the opponent will fall to this side.

Fifty Nine.
Counter the reverse belt & go to ground:

This technique uses the mechanics of the prior method, but here **B** grabs just one of the opponent's arms, one hand at the wrist and the other on the elbow, passing from under **A** and to the outside.

Sixty.

Counter the head hold:

    A passes his right arm over to encircle the head of **B**. **B** replies by putting his right arm on **A**'s head and passing his left hand under to grab hold of **A**'s left shoulder.

Sixty One.
Counter the head hold:

Having taken hold of **B**'s head by passing his right arm over it, **B** drops to his right knee and places his left hand on the right elbow of **A**, forcing the opponent to go down with him. From here **B** passes his right arm between the legs of **A**, hooking the lower part of **A**'s right leg and dragging it toward him.

Sixty Two.
Counter the head hold:

As with technique 60, save that instead of grabbing **A**'s right shoulder, **B** reaches between the opponent's legs to hook a thigh.

B might also opt for a lower hold rather than grabbing the thigh.

Another counter would include **B** forgoing the head and arm hold, belting the opponent with his right arm which he passes under **A**'s left arm, and replacing the underhook on the left thigh with an overhook of the right thigh with his left arm.

This move is indicated as a counter, but of course it can also be used as an attack.

Sixty Three.
Head and shoulder hold with trip:

B is leaning forward with his upper body and **A** passes his left arm under to seize the right shoulder, placing his right hand on the nape of **B**'s neck and spinning him to the right as he throws his left leg out to block the left leg of **B**.

Sixty Four.

Head and shoulder hold with a sweep:

Just as in 63, but here the blocking leg is replaced with an active sweep which **A** applies with his right leg low and to the inside of **B**'s right leg.

Sixty Five.

Feign the arm drag & apply forearm to chin, plus counter.

A shoves his right forearm beneath the chin of **B,** forcing his head back. At the same time **A** spins left, passing his right arm over the right arm of **B** to apply the arm drag shown in 18 and 19.

To counter this movement, **B** will shove A's right arm away with his left elbow, then drop to snag the **A**'s leg as shown in the following technique.

Sixty Six.
Front crotch lift:

A drops his stance, either following the attack shown in 65 or after having dragged the opponent's arm by the wrist. He then encircles **B**'s thigh and lifts him.

B feels himself being hoisted and encircles the head of **A** who lifts him higher, passing his right arm between the legs. **A** seeks to push his arms through as fully as possible in order to take **B** down to the rear in a supine position.

The move also serves as a counter to the reverse head hold, though it can be used on its own without hooking the head.

A lifts **B** in the manner described in 66 and 67. Instead of (as in 66) bumping the rear of the knee, **A** releases the left hand in order to grab the right wrist of **B**. Maintaining the lift with his right arm, **A** pulls the opponent to the right in order to load him onto his hip.

Sixty Nine.
Following the thigh lift:

A hoists **B** up by the thigh as per 66, lifting him as high as possible and bringing him to the horizontal position. **A** releases his right hand in order to hook the left arm of **B** from the outside and above. **A** turns **B** in front of him. In practice **A** should reduce the impact of **B**'s fall by bending his knees and going to ground with the opponent.

This technique can be linked to 45 (**B**).

Just as in the prior technique, save that instead of seizing the arm, **A** places his right hand on the nape of **B**'s neck and causes him to fall.

Instead of simply placing his hand on the back of **B**'s neck, **A** can encircle the head with his arm.

Seventy One.
Counter the thigh lift:

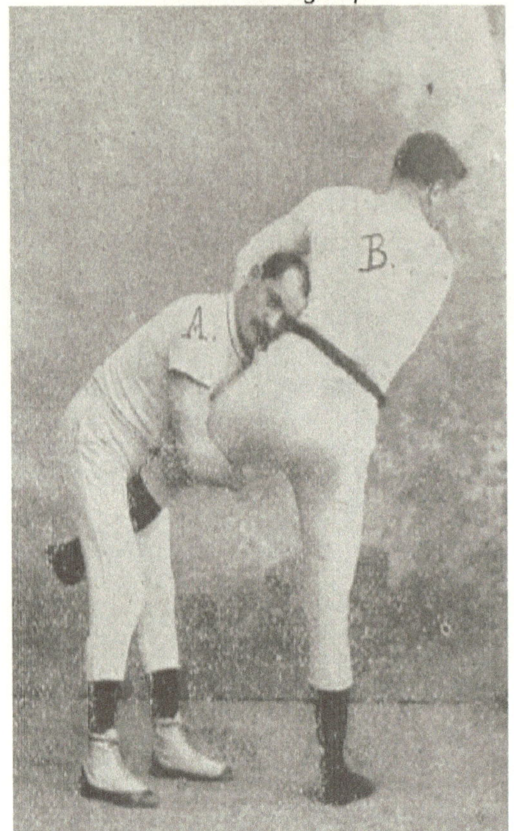

First **A** hooks the left thigh of **B** in the manner indicated in 65 and 66. **B** sets his left leg between those of **A**.

Continuing on, **B** falls to his hands and sets his right leg outside of the right leg of **A**. **B** then spins to the left on his own axis.

If this does not meet with success, **B** will at least be able to compromise the balance of his opponent.

Seventy Three.
Hooking the leg to counter the thigh lift:

A snags the right leg of **B** who must then set the leg between those of the attacker. **B** grabs the right leg of **A** with his left hand below the knee and inside and his right hand grabbing it from the above and outside.

With his right elbow shoving into the opponent, **B** then spins to the right.

Leg & head hold as a counter to the thigh hold:

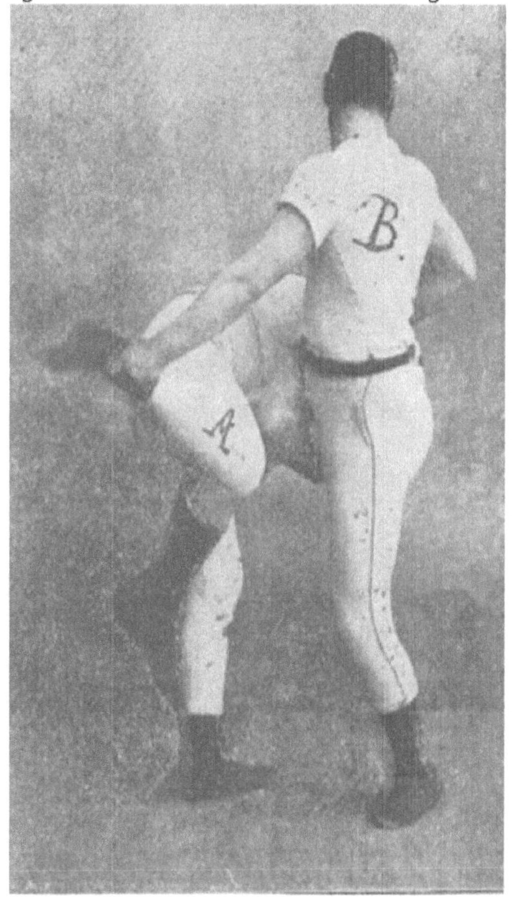

Just as in technique 73, but here, instead of seizing the thigh with his right hand, **B** places it on the nape of **A**'s neck and spins quickly to the right. His left hand grabs the instep of **A**'s right leg and pulls it up, forcing it to bend.

Seventy Five.
Belt and leg hold as a counter to the thigh hold:

Just as in the prior technique, but instead of placing his right hand on the back of the opponent's neck, **B** belts **A** with his right arm, as **B**'s left leg is not detached from the mat.

Seventy Six.

Belt with leg hold, falling to a knee to counter a thigh hold:

Just as in 75, but instead of grabbing **A**'s right instep **B** passes his left arm *under* to snag the left instep, raising the leg and causing it to bend before dropping to his right knee.

Seventy Seven.

Counter a thigh grab:

    A grabs the thigh of **B.** **B** bends his right leg to trap the **A**'s arms between his calf and thigh, then slips his right arm over and his left arm under the opponent's waist, joining them beneath the opponent's belt and lifting to tumble him.

Seventy Eight.
Shoulder hold and trip:

    B leans forward looking to grab a thigh, and **A** passes his right arm under **B**'s left and his left arm over it, exerting pressure with his left elbow and turning to spin **B** while **A**'s left foot sweeps **B**'s right leg from the outside.

    This move can also work without the sweep.

Seventy Nine.

Lift through an ankle grab or following a thigh grab:

If **A** succeeds in getting to the side of **B** he belts the opponent up with his right arm and dips to grab his ankle from the inside.

From the position described above, **A** can bring his opponent down through the techniques shown in 34, 56, 62, 69, and 70.

B can also be taken down to the left by a right hip throw (see 52).

<h1 style="text-align:center">Eighty.</h1>

Takedown through overhook and crotch lift:

After lifting **A** by grabbing a thigh or ankle, or having dislodged an inside hook (see 45), **B** brings the opponent to the ground and maintains his hold on the right leg, then lifts it quickly after having passed his left arm between **A**'s legs. His right arm goes over the opponent and **B** locks his hands. Pressing with his right arm forces the torso of **A** down, facilitating his fall.

B can also spin in order to take **A** down.

Eighty One.

Thigh grab feint to take an arm, topple opponent with a trip.

    B turns his right side to **A** who passes his left arm between **B**'s legs, securing a thigh. **B** seeks to make him let go, and **A** takes advantage of this: As soon **B**'s right arm comes close to his own left hand to grab it, **A** places his right arm over it while with his right foot he sweeps the right leg of **B**.

    This technique can also be performed with **A** seizing **B**'s right arm with both hands and drawing it to him, placing it between **B**'s legs. **A** lets go quickly with his left to grab **B**'s wrist from behind, and passes his right arm over. 81 shows the manner in which to continue.

B places his hands on the nape of **A**'s neck. **A** grabs **B**'s left wrist with his right hand, and with his left hand he secures the opponent's right arm above the elbow.

Having raised **B**'s right arm, **A** spins to the right while his left hand slides to grab the right wrist of the opponent.

Eighty Four.

Double arm hold III:

Continuing his spin to the right, **A** crosses the right arm of **B** over the left and ducks under them to load the opponent up and then drop him.

Eighty Five.
Arm drag and sweep:

    A places his left forearm under the chin of **B**, his left hand at the left shoulder. **A** then grabs the opponent's right arm above the elbow with his right hand and, setting his left foot behind **B**'s right leg, he drags **B**'s right foot off of the mat while pulling hard with his right and shoving into the opponent with his forearm. If **B** is not forced onto his back, he will at least be unbalanced.

Eighty Six.
The Bridge:

The bridge serves as a counter to many attacks. Your body weight comes to rest on your head and the soles of your feet, which are set apart.

To collapse the bridge one must pass the right arm over the right of the opponent and bring the hand behind the head insofar as is possible. Apply pressure and pass in front with a leap to force the head to forward. Use your left arm to help, placing it at the nape of the neck.

Another way to proceed is to mount the opponent and pass your legs inside of his before forcing his legs apart.

Eighty Seven.
Grounded arm and leg hold:

After getting to **B**'s right side, **A** passes his right arm under the right arm of **B** and overhooks his left. With his left hand **A** grabs **B**'s right leg at the instep. **A** presses his chin into the back of **B** and rolls him.

Instead of grabbing the right leg with his left hand **A** can grab the left arm.

A could also opt to seize the left thigh with an underhook, passing his arm between the legs of the opponent.

After having gained the right side of **B**, **A** grabs the right leg with his hands, his right arm overhooking, the left underhooking. He lifts and stands up straight, then passes his left leg between those of the opponent while slipping under the raised leg, placing behind the left leg of **B**. He pulls with this leg and throws himself forward to roll **B**. Before throwing himself forward **A** can choose to belt **B** with a right overhook.

Eighty Eight.
Grounded neck and thigh hold:

Having taken **B**'s left side, **A** passes his left arm under the left arm of **B** and hooks his neck. He passes his right arm down beneath the opponent's legs and grabs the right thigh, rolling **B** forward.

Eighty Nine.
Takedown with a neck hold, thigh to the ground:

Just as in the prior technique but here **A** lifts **B** to cause his fall. **A** takes care to push hard on the nape of **B**'s neck, but it is best to set the attacking hand on the crown of the head.

Ninety.

Counter a neck underhook on the ground:

As soon as **A** passes his right arm under the right arm of **B** in order to set his hand on **B**'s neck, **B** places his left hand to the outside of **A**'s right knee and hooks **A**'s right arm with his own right arm, then he spins to the right.

Ninety One.
Hook the thigh and arm on the ground:

With his right arm **A** seizes the right arm of **B** at the wrist from the inside in order to squeeze the arm tight to him. With his left arm he hooks the right thigh. **A** rotates to the left and lifts **B** with his right arm.

The thigh hold can be executed before the arm hold. After trapping the arm **A** can seek to seize the right wrist of **B** who will be located between the arms.

Ninety Two.
Shoulder hold on the ground.

A passes his left arm under the left arm of **B** then over **B**'s back in order to grab the shoulder. His right arm passes under and then that hand also seizes **B**'s right shoulder. **A** applies pressure with his left arm and pulls with his right hand.

Ninety Three.
Side belt and arm throw on the ground:

A belts **B** with his right arm and loads him onto his right hip. He raises **B** up while with his left hand and shoves **B**'s left arm away in order to spin him to the right, controlling his shoulders.

Ninety Four.

Turning the opponent with a thigh hold on the ground:

A grabs **B**'s right thigh while passing his left arm to the inside. He rises to a full stand and loads the opponent onto his left hip. **A** pushes with his right elbow to keep **B** from turning at the moment he is being taken down. **B** is overturned with a spin.

It is best if **A** keeps the opponent tight to him.

If **B** seeks to turn, **A** can lift him up while turning at the same time, which is to say that he may turn several times on his own axis.

Ninety Five.

Overturning opponent with spin & thigh hold, sweeping the arms.

Just as in the previous technique, but here **A** sweeps the right arm of **B** with his right foot while the spin is occuring.

Before executing the arm sweep, player **A** should seek to lift his opponent to avoid fracturing the attacked arm.

Ninety Six.
Overturning opponent with thigh hold, arm trip.

Just as in 94 and 95 but here as **A** rises up he places his left leg in front of the right arm of **B** who is then overturned after **A** loads him onto his left hip and then dumps him via rotation.

In this position, **A** should never send his opponent directly forward as it would be very dangerous. Remember that the opponent must be loaded onto the hip.

Overturning with a flip, thigh hold on the ground:

Just as in 94, once the opponent is lifted **A** releases his right hand and pushes on the back of **B**'s neck to flip him.

It is better to place a hand on the crown of the head. This move can be done without loading the opponent onto your hip.

Ninety Eight.

Counter a lift with a thigh hold on the ground:

Passing his left arm outside and his right arm inside, **A** grabs **B** by a thigh to lift him. **B** drops his weight and places his right hand over the left elbow of **B** to immobilize that arm while putting his left leg up against **A**'s right. **B** puts his head to the mat and draws **A** to him while taking care to lift his left leg at the same moment the right leg of **A** is detached from the mat.

B can also take hold of **A**'s left leg with his left hand.

Ninety Nine.
Between the legs lift with foot to the back.

Once **B** is inverted and **A** finds himself between the opponent's legs, he grabs both thighs and lifts the opponent. **B**'s hands go to the mat, and **A** passes his right leg over **B**'s back before spinning to the left to take **B** down.

It is essential that **B**'s legs are lifted as high as possible and held tight to the body.